the hamptons

the hamptons
life behind the hedges

by Susan P. Meisel and Ellen Harris

photographs by Susan P. Meisel

Harry N. Abrams, Inc., Publishers

editor: **Ruth A. Peltason**
designer: **Ana Rogers**

PAGE 1: Sagg Main Street is an American country classic. Fortunately for us it still remains so today. This 300-year-old homestead is sacred to Sagaponack.

PAGES 2-3: On a village lane in East Hampton a quiet mood is created by this wall of arborvitae.

Photographs on pages 55, 66 left, 67 right, 68, 69, 70 top, 131, 132 left, 134, 136, and 137 are by Steve Lopez, Logo Studios.

Library of Congress Cataloging-in-Publication Data

Meisel, Susan Pear
The Hamptons: life behind the hedges / by Susan P. Meisel and Ellen Harris
p. cm.
ISBN 0−8109−3431−0
I. Hamptons (N.Y.)—Pictorial works.
2. Dwellings—New York (State)—Hamptons—Pictorial works.
3. Interior architecture—New York (State)—Hamptons—Pictorial works.
4. Landscape—New York (State)—Hamptons—Pictorial works.
5. Hamptons (N.Y.)—Social life and customs—Pictorial works.
I. Harris, Ellen, 1946– II. Title.
F127.S9 M45   2000
974.7'25–dc21   99−462336

Printed and bound in Japan

Harry N. Abrams, Inc.
100 Fifth Avenue
New York, N.Y. 10011
www.abramsbooks.com

contents

acknowledgments

As this was a first book for both of us we didn't know what to expect or what was expected of us. The biggest problem for us was the editing process. So we left it to our editor, Ruth Peltason, whose flawless eye and editorial acumen made the process painless and pleasurable. And we looked to our book designer, Ana Rogers, whose design talent pulled it all together. We feel the end result reflects the Hamptons we love . . . and so we say thank you to both our editor and designer without whom this book would not have been made possible. We are particularly grateful to Paul Gottlieb for believing in this project.

To all the homeowners who so generously opened their homes and gardens and allowed us to photograph we say thank you. Special thanks to Steve Lopez, who helped with photography and who taught me not to be afraid of picking up a camera and having a good time with it. (SPM) We're grateful to the artists who allowed us to photograph in their studios: Ross Bleckner, Chuck Close, Audrey Flack, Jan Freilicher, Steve Miller, and Susan Nash.

Thanks also to the following for their special help along the way: Barbara and Sean Bailey, Susan Beckman and Robert Barandes, Peter Chervin, Leslie and Chuck Close, Michael and Eileen Friedman, Joan Gelman, Nancy Grigor, Donna Karan and her assistant Susie Lish, Allen and Robin Kopelson, Ngaere Macrae, Jimmy and Iris Marden, Jane and Richard Novick, Elizabeth Barlow Rogers, Martin and Susan Schulman, Joy Schwartzman, Gil Shapiro and Judith Stockman, Ellen Sosnow, Martha Stewart, Connie and Jeff Tarrant, Gary and Nina Wexler, Toby Wienberger, Peri Wolfman and Charles Gold.

To our husbands: Louis Meisel, who has taught me many great lessons about life besides the appreciation of beautiful things; and to Brian Harris, my biggest fan in life besides my friend Susan—for his critiques always softened by his mirth, and his lawyerly influence of reminding me often about brevity with words.

This book is dedicated to the great loves of our lives Louis, Ari, and Brian.

Susan P. Meisel
Ellen Harris
Sagaponack, New York, 1999

All things blue: the ticking, the floral cushion, even the owner's dog, aptly named Blue after his favorite color.

PAGE 6: Preserving the dune . . . a snow fence zigzags its way down a Sagaponack beach.

PAGE 7: A boardwalk cuts through the marsh toward Mecox Bay.

A recently built Easthampton house reinterprets the classic Shingle Style.

Reminiscent of a Hopper landscape.

BELOW: It's a dog's life.

introduction

If you are fortunate enough to experience the beach as a young person then you never forget the sound and smell of the ocean, the warmth of the sand, and the starry nights. It's a memory that's refreshed each time you go back to the beach. It's a memory that never grows old.

The process of winding down, of thinking about the beach and the pleasure of being surrounded by so much natural beauty, begins as you are heading out of the city, knowing that your destination is one of pure relaxation. It's a wonderful feeling. It isn't necessary for there to be blue skies and sunshine for you to enjoy yourself at the beach. What's essential is getting there and then staying as long as possible. The Hamptons are like precious few places these days.

It was in this magical part of the eastern end of Long Island that we met and discovered how similar our passions are. Since childhood, we had each spent most of our summers at the beach. And, as it turned out, we had each harbored the dream to one day own beach houses as adults. Fortunately, that dream has come true, and with it all the fun and real joy of being in one of the country's most special places.

One day two summers ago we were driving down a road in Sagaponack that runs parallel to the ocean. We were mesmerized by the incredible vista: The ocean was sparkling, the sky was mixed with extraordinary shades of blue, the fields were filled with nodding sunflowers, and the privet hedges were monstrous. The walls of privet were surrounding houses we remembered from some time ago but could no longer see. When had the privet grown so tall? And what was it hiding?

A beautiful example of an American cast-iron fence with original paint, circa 1874.

As we drove around, we kept saying, "Look at those hedges, look at the house behind those hedges. Look, look, look." And then, inevitably, the question "What's inside that house?" came to mind. We figured that there must be many other people who have wondered the same thing, and it was at that moment that the idea for this book was born. We decided to document in pictures and words our definition of living in the Hamptons and to create this book as a way of capturing our feeling about being here. We hoped our book would become a keepsake of the very best of the Hamptons, or at the very least a scrapbook of our affection for this remarkable place, especially the area in and around Sagaponack, where we each have family homes. We hope that whenever you want to visit, or revisit, the Hamptons, you have only to open this book and travel with us along the back roads, beaches, and hidden drives, and enter the world "behind the hedges."

The Hamptons we love are, firstly, the summer months . . . the time to enjoy it all. It's when your days off are all the more special. For most of us, it's vacation time. And it's also when visitors who come here discover what we have known for a long time—that the Hamptons are a special place. Come September, summer residents go home, town empties out, and everything gets much quieter. It's these autumn days when the weather cools that we're reminded of the holidays to come . . . it's the time of gray-blue skies with breaks of yellow sunshine. Winter is a time to explore all those places you couldn't really see before. And of course in the spring everything wakes up, and with spring comes the knowledge that summer is but a skip away.

There is no imitation for living in the Hamptons. The house you live in may be a small and cozy cottage or one of the grand "potato mansions" sprouting in the once-potato fields of yester-day. Your house may be a former utilitarian farm building—albeit in an easily recognizable barn, horse stable, potting shed, or chicken coop—or maybe it's an architect's dream. Whatever your pleasure and whatever the size of your budget, in the Hamptons you can be the magician.

The Hamptons have been such a big part of our lives. In this book we've tried to share what we love about this stretch of Long Island, from Southampton to Shelter Island to Montauk, too, and the many villages in between. For us, the Hamptons have the right ingredients: a little bit of fluff to make it interesting, and a lot of the real thing to make it inviting. This is where everybody loves the familiar landscape—the big sky, the long, white stretches of beach, and the country living edged by closeness of the ocean. It's the best of many worlds and a place to enjoy every day of the year.

Whoever said "take time to smell the roses" could have been at the beach because once you have sand in your shoes you never want to get it out.

The Hamptons at sunset — superlatives almost seem superflous

behind
the hedges

Hamptons' hedges are in a league of their own. The hedges, or privet as it is known in these parts, are fashioned into tall clipped walls or left to grow big and bushy. Historically, privet was all about privacy and enclosing the property from the outside world. It entices the passerby to wonder what lies beyond. The living green wall doesn't shout "no trespassing"; instead it softly and lushly reminds us to respect others' personal time.

Step behind these walls and you are stepping into a time where past and present coexist. The focus changes. The sounds of the road are muffled. Birdsong is more distinct. The sweet smell of the flowers is more intense. Above all, the house comes into view. Even the most humble abode is enhanced when sheltered behind tall hedges. In the landscape designers' world, hedges create "good bones." More than a cultivated boundary, hedges give protection from the wind so that the property can be planned for a variety of uses. With the wind tamed to a gentle breeze, a June perennial garden can be counted on each year to welcome in the summer. And if you want to live close to the sea, the privet is planted more out of necessity than any other reason, although there are many great reasons for this greenery.

There are so many choices for creating a hedge. Privet is the premiere plant matter in the Hamptons. Deciduous in nature, privet can still hold its leaves throughout most of the year. In the short days of winter there is something pleasing about the twiglike branches revealing an outline of its former self. There is another reward if you are here during those very cold days. You get to see what the privet has hidden during the lush months of summer. It's somewhat out of focus but clear enough to entice during a casual drive or bicycle ride. With their centuries-long history of gardening, the English use that most wonderful of all 'Fagus sylvatica'. . . European beech. Homeowners in the Hamptons who long to surround themselves with this type of hedge find out early on that they have a very long wait to create sizeable beech walls. Fortunately, privet is not the only choice for good hedge material. Fitzer junipers, red-winged euonymus,

PREVIOUS SPREAD: Wonderfully pleasing to the eye! A wall of privet dresses up a gravel driveway.

mop-head hydrangeas, fairy roses, false cypress, cryptomeria, and even stands of bamboo all make for great hedges. But it is the eponymous privet hedges in the villages of Southampton and Easthampton, majestic in size and shape, that characterize the communities of the South Fork.

The farmland towns of Sagaponack, Bridgehampton, and Wainscott have hedges that are a more informal part of the landscape. The privet blossoms are left on to attract birds and butterflies. When the hedges are grown with abandon a great deal of space is necessary. An informal hedge needs much more room to grow wider than it is high. If you listen you can almost hear it growing.

If you have that special ingredient that is good Bridgehampton loam, then you are very fortunate and so is your hedge. If you do not have the perfect soil then it can be amended with compost, peat moss, and vitamins. Follow with plenty of TLC and water, water, and more water. In a few years time the newly planted hedge will blend with all the shades of green. Even the careful observer will have a difficult time telling old privet from new. Privet of all sorts is a trademark of living in the Hamptons.

Southampton privet at its finest. These hedges took years of growing and years of masterful pruning.

OPPOSITE: A classically clipped arbor creates a walkway between the artistically designed hedges. Beyond, old trees protect a perfect place for a shade garden.

RIGHT: The hedge structure is a perfect resting place for the companionship of clematis paniculata. This is a late-blooming vine that flowers in early September.

BELOW: Roses run rampant up a long pergola making a romantic walkway from one garden room to the other.

Years of growing and a great sense of humor carved this huge ball of privet.

RIGHT: An arbor of clematis paniculata is a charming way to divide the main grounds leading to the guest house. Here the clematis has been trained to grow over an arbor that anchors a late-blooming garden of Russian sage, lithrum, and sedum.

Deceptively simple, yet manicured and cared for to perfection. A curved privet divides the driveway from the main house.

LEFT: The crowning of a cottage.

in the front door and out the back

The intrigue of what is behind the hedges begins as you follow the path to the front door. You might walk on old brick, stone, flagstone, pebbles, gravel, grass, or the like. The path can be bordered by any combination of perennials, annuals, and shrubs, or just simply edged with grass. Each house creates its own special outdoor mood. What surrounds the house in the country is equally as important as what goes on inside.

Usually the style of the inside is somewhat reflected by what you see on the outside. We photographed an artist's house and studio. The house was the ultimate in simplicity, no clutter, and with great taste. Everything was chosen to create a specific mood. The mood suggested perfection. Everything had a place and everything was in its place. The surrounding grounds suggested the same feeling—all was perfectly ordered, nothing was out of context. Not a single leaf or flower where it didn't belong. In the home of a noted antique dealer and designer the rooms were filled with collections of all sorts representing years of careful purchases. The collecting didn't stop at the entranceway, but continued out back with the same passion as inside. There, several stone statues dotted the grounds around the house. Two stone dobermans guarded an entranceway outdoors. A bronze dolphin sprayed water, making music on the usually quiet pool. Each piece was given the space and importance it deserved, representing the eclectic collecting spirit of its owners. And then there was the home of a famous clothing designer, where everything was dressed in white, conveying peace and tranquility. This paradise spilled onto the outdoor meditation room, complete with a prayer bench and Buddha shrine. A strategically placed outdoor shower was so inviting we wanted to strip naked and jump right in! The strict adherence to the color white extended to the entire garden, from the shrubs to the flowering plants. The deliberate simplicity of the front entrance gave way to the calming fantasy land that claimed one of the most spectacular open bay views in the Hamptons.

Each house we visited, some grand, some simple, all created their own special style. We were never disappointed and were always inspired.

PREVIOUS SPREAD: A Sagaponack home stands majestic in a large former potato field surrounded by working farmland. It's also close enough to the water to hear the pounding surf and feel the breeze off the ocean.

Some say that this weeping beech in Easthampton is the largest of its kind on the East End.

A rustic house on the ocean in Sagaponack created from an eclectic mix of vernacular structures, sheds, barns, and one-room dwellings.

A pair of dogs stand watch at this Greek Revival–style house in Sag Harbor.

A quintessential turn-of-the-century Shelter Island summerhouse viewed from the water.

This little gem of a New England saltbox is beloved by its Jefferson Street neighbors in Sag Harbor.

We pass this Victorian home just about every time we go to one of our favorite beaches. For the Fourth of July, its owners decorate it high to low with American flags. The flowering hostas that line the path always make us smile.

The iron gate in front of this Sag Harbor Federal home, dating from the early 1900s,
is a perfect example of the lasting heritage of this old whaling village.

simple
pleasures

It may be the new American dream. Everything races by at such a fast pace. It's hard to keep up and, ironically, if you can it gets harder to enjoy what counts. As we move further ahead we long to look back to a simpler time to cherish the simple pleasures. As we sit here and write about simple pleasures we look out the window and never tire of what we see. We ride our bikes down a private dirt road and walk up a short path over the dune to a white sand beach with one of the best views on the East Coast.

The beach becomes the place for special moments. How many times have we dragged bags laden with books, magazines, and newspapers only to drag the same bags back home, neither looked at nor touched. It is always with good intentions that we arrive at the beach with pads of paper, bags stuffed with notes ready to write, but instead nature wins out—the warm sand, the rhythm of the ocean, the aroma of the clean summer air takes over. Forget the writing, forget the reading; we are incapable of performing. Ours is a euphoria that incapacitates. As the day passes, the beach scene becomes a composition in motion. The day people depart and the evening performance begins. People start arriving to prepare for their evening barbecues. The fishermen arrive, cast their lines, settle in, and wait. The families appear with their kids, dogs in tow, carrying their picnic baskets laden with the evening supper. Days like these give us memories to live on and the knowledge that sometimes the simple pleasures are what life is all about.

The sign on this gate says it all!

PREVIOUS SPREAD: A real working farm in Wainscott is an example of the vanishing landscape. We looked at this setting and felt that time was standing still.

The perfect hammock.

A wonderful example of a handmade rustic bench.

What fun it was to discover this antique weathered Coca-Cola bench in the backyard of this Bridgehampton house.

A group of foxgloves in a shade garden filled with ferns.

RIGHT: A wrought-iron bench no longer used for seating has become an ivy-covered still life in a peaceful corner of a Wainscott garden.

BELOW: Every year we ride our bikes on the annual Bridgehampton house tour. This year we got lost and found ourselves biking up a steep roadway. There we discovered the best seats in the house to admire the ocean view.

RIGHT: While we were visiting a friend in Amagansett last summer, we looked out the main door to the beach and there they were, these three old friends. We knew we had to take a picture. We were watching them watch the sky, the ocean, and the beach. They were mesmerized and so were we.

Shelter Island from the water.

A sleepy sailboat rests on Great Peconic Bay.

This enchanting white-washed shed is situated on a direct route to the beach.

LEFT: Homage to the red, white, and blue.

Memories of our childhood . . . the old-fashioned swing is still the best.

LEFT: The preservation of this vintage barn becomes the focal point in the backyard of a charming village house in Southampton.

An artist's paradise.

The real McCoy: A working farm in Sagaponack.

An alfresco dinner party in Watermill.

The perfect setting.

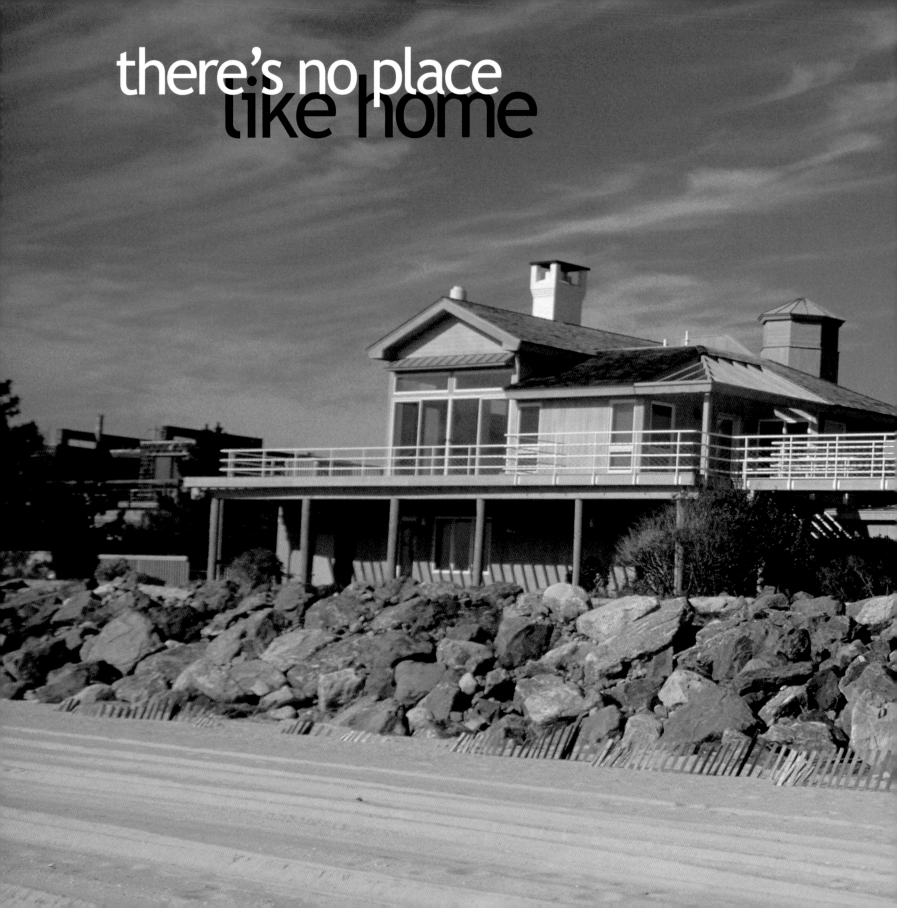

Coming home to the country is about a **lifestyle** that is like no other. People come here to relax and it shows by how they live. In a sense, there are two kinds of Hamptons. There is the Hamptons *scene*: the over-the-top glitzy Hamptons we read about in the newspapers and magazines, with the latest buzz about the parties, the restaurants, the social scene. Then there is the other Hamptons, what we think of as *our* Hamptons: good times spent at home with family and friends. These are the days to make the moments count.

Ask yourself to describe what a house in the Hamptons means. The word **peaceful** is what first comes to mind. Then add to this list *fresh, summer, views, light, fun, friends, food,* and *great happiness.* The good times at the beach are what makes going there worthwhile—it's a world beyond pretense and attitude. In the Hamptons, it's the blend of country charm and beach living that anchors the modern beach house with its more traditional shingled-clad neighbors. In the past the Hamptons were anything but decorated. You were at the beach, life was carefree, and the look was **casual.** Family cast-offs short on design but long on comfort were the rule. Even though location, architecture, and design play a much more important role today, the emphasis is still on simplicity, relaxation, and comfort. Sometimes even the birds have a well-designed house to come home to. After all, it's still the Hamptons!

Once home, most people choose a favorite room. If you are a weekend chef the kitchen becomes the place to gather. Conversation is easy over a great dinner with good friends. The living room might have a favorite chair to settle in and read a good book, or you just might walk outside, pull up a lounge chair, and daydream. Whatever your pleasure, and whatever time of the day or night, it is a spiritual experience to throw open the doors and let the fragrant cross breezes of summer fill the rooms. **Comfort** is the operative word. Your feet are up, your mind is at ease, and nothing feels like it can go wrong. Life is good. There's no place like home.

Beach-front tennis in Watermill. It's been there forever!

RIGHT: Living at the edge of the sea has its risks. A Sagaponack house is forced to retreat after a hard winter.

PREVIOUS SPREAD: A Sagaponack beach house protected by a beautiful stone embankment.

The only thing better than a clean, perfectly tidied kitchen is one that has all the spills and other tell-tale signs of the makings of a good meal.

The dried hydrangeas came from the owner's garden.

BELOW: Shades of white are the peaceful palette for this fashion designer's home.

An artist creates her own still life from her cutting garden in Bridgehampton.

Deceptively simple and sublime: instead of an overabundance of charm, this Bridgehapmton bedroom is an oasis of calm.

It may look overgrown to a purist, but clearly the owner of this small Sag Harbor cottage has taken a page straight out of a nineteenth-century gardening book.

A cutting garden, a weathered gray bench, and a pergola with a view—looks pretty inviting to us.

When this trumpet vine blooms in August the chimney piece is ablaze with orange flowers. Incredibly, the vine naturally took the shape of the chimney without spreading to the rest of the house.

Topiary is the operative word for this French-inspired property. Also impressive is the formal rose garden with its sheared green walls.

A pool house cottage surrounded by fall foliage.

OPPOSITE: This timeless Sag Main Street house has a massive hydrangea tree that has been growing for years. Florabunda at its finest.

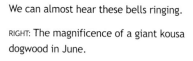

We can almost hear these bells ringing.

RIGHT: The magnificence of a giant kousa dogwood in June.

A shade garden of ferns, abelia, lady's mantle, and peonies.

Beautifully pruned rows of young hydrangea trees soften the entranceway to this Sagaponack house.

A flagstone path to the tennis court is bordered by grasses and black-eyed Susans, both easy plants to grow in the summer by the seashore.

LEFT: Windswept seaside garden of ornamental grasses and silver-leafed caryopteris grow happily side by side in the August heat. Even at its hottest—and August in New York can be very hot—the Hamptons are blessed by their proximity to the ocean.

fields of
dreams

Who doesn't want to wake up each morning, throw open the windows, and look out at the view? This is the first thing to do when you are in the Hamptons. You feel alive with the breeze at your face, its sweetness mingling with the sound of the waves, however distant they may be. That breezy, salty air seduces us to get outside and surround ourselves with any open space near at hand. It doesn't take long to find these chosen spots and admire the rituals of this onetime extensive farming community.

The dry winter fields soon give way to the farmers on their tractors creating perfectly spaced lines in freshly plowed dirt. As summer progresses the fields emerge full blown: Depending on the season, you can find asparagus, broccoli, lettuce, brussels sprouts, potatoes, leeks, peaches, pears, apples, strawberries, and raspberries. The list is endless. The close of summer signals the autumn harvest of pumpkins. Out on the East End, the tomato crop is big business and the array impressive. Big red and yellow tomatoes, quirky looking heirloom tomatoes, tiny little pear tomatoes . . . whatever your pleasure, you'll find farm stands all along the Hamptons stocked with just-picked still-warm tomatoes. If you have ever had the thrill of running through a cornfield you'll remember the sounds, the smells, and the tickle of the corn husks (Been-here-forever cornfields are reminiscent of playing hide-and-seek during the summers of childhood.) Hopefully you had the good sense to freeze a baker's dozen of corn when the days are short and cold.

The changing landscape is studded with houses surrounded by perfectly clipped gardens and manicured hedges, but nothing is as pleasurable as seeing the remaining views of the open fields brimming with wildflowers, corn, and rows upon rows of sunflowers. And given the proximity of the water, perhaps most breathtaking of all is watching the fields fill with the mist rolling in from the sea. The light changes, quiet fills the air, and you realize how lucky we are to have these fields of dreams.

Yes, a few unspoiled places do remain.

The nodding heads of a field of sunflowers follow the sun.

An enviable wave of violet-tinged allium in a June garden.

OPPOSITE: The yellow lets you imagine this as a field of sunshine.

A poolside view of the potato fields that run all the way to the ocean.

LEFT: This field of cosmos reseeds itself each year.

It's pretty elementary: sky, wheat, and corn.

OPPOSITE, TOP: Not a template for a Japanese dry garden, but the whorls of the wheat thresher.

OPPOSITE, BOTTOM: Remember the lines, "The corn is as high as an elephant's eye. You can almost hear it growing."

A field of corn is bordered by a corridor of wheat.

Form, function, and beauty.

These three silos remind us of the way it used to be.

RIGHT: When the Sagaponack fog rolls in off the ocean
it's not unusual to have visibility cut to just a few feet.

for the love
of blue

The color blue in the Hamptons comes in so many shapes and sizes it is hard not to look somewhere and say how much you love the color blue. The dictionary definition is so descriptive of the Hamptons one would think that Noah Webster himself was visiting here when he wrote the definition, "Having the color of the clear blue sky or the deep sea." Blue is the definitive color of summer in the Hamptons. Whoever forgets going down to the beach and marveling at the vastness of the blue sky and the endless vista of the blue ocean? Driving around the Hamptons you can see dozens of shades of blue that appear not only outdoors but inside on tables, in living rooms, and in artists' studios. Regardless of how a house is designed, any house in the Hamptons is inspired by the big sky and the closeness of the sea.

One day when we drove down to the ocean we were especially struck by the blueness of the water. The sun, beating down on the sand, was causing a mirrorlike effect on the waves. We walked into the ocean and as we began taking pictures the water changed color from midnight blue to almost black. The huge sky was clear without a single cloud and blue as blue could be. During the winter months we can actually visualize walking on the beach that day in Sagaponack and remembering where the sky and the ocean met. . . . All blue!

June gardens throughout the Hamptons show off the blue palette to perfection. All summer long there are antique shows, flea markets, and tag sales. Piles of blue-and-white ticking, stacks of blue-and-white platters, paintings of blue sky and blue-flowered gardens satisfy the blue-and-white urges in all of us. One day while out photographing we happened to be lucky enough to see various shades of blue hydrangeas as far as the eye could see. Whoever said "I'm feeling blue" should have picked another color.

PREVIOUS SPREAD: View from Bridge Lane—springtime over Sagaponack Pond with twin crab apple trees in bloom.

Town Line Beach the day before a big hurricane.

Mother Nature at work. Picture perfect.

Where Southampton Town meets Easthampton Town at Town Line Beach.

A painter's sky!

The glory of summer—masses of blue hydrangeas.

Blue veronica edges the path in a private June garden in Southampton Village.

A pool with a view overlooking 36 acres of flat Sagaponack farmland and the surf in the background.

The blue of the sky, the water, the flowers, and the finishing touch of blue in the painted shutters highlight this shingled house in Wainscott.

Rudbeckia hirta, commonly called black-eyed Susan, is an easy plant to grow in the Hamptons. It's also terrific in contrast with blue.

BELOW: She's in charge of product design for a well-known company and he is a famous food photographer; together their country home in Watermill reflects their superb taste.

Looking toward Peters Pond Beach, Sagaponack.

Winter surf in Sagaponack.

RIGHT: White sail, blue water—a perfect day.

The fabled lighthouse in Montauk overlooks a rock-strewn shoreline.

See Spot look for the fire truck!

Montauk, the easternmost town on Long Island, stretches out toward Europe. It has been said that the rocks are so precious, no one is allowed to take any as souvenirs.

Yet another terrific Hamptons weekend antique show.

LEFT: Vintage luggage recycled and used not only for travel, but stacked and used for end tables and coffee tables.

RIGHT: Great storage possibilities.

Ticking is usually thought of as being blue-and-white like a mattress. This red-and-khaki ticking shows a beautiful alternative.

OPPOSITE: Small colorful hook rugs make a statement on bare wood floors—or even on the grass at this antique fair.

Vintage ticking in color schemes for everyone's palate.

OPPOSITE: Beacon and Pendleton blankets from the 1930s and 40s were manufactured in Canada and the Northwest. Their sturdiness, warmth, and wonderful range of colors make them as popular today as when they were first made. Designers have even adapted them for casual sportswear.

obsessions —
less is more but
more is better

Flotsam from the neighbors yard sale. Going junking two ferry rides away. Tag sales, dealers showcasing their wares at local antique shows, the auctions, and the shopping in Easthampton, Bridgehampton, Southampton, and Sag Harbor. You can easily lose track of time while looking to expand your current collection. What was a hobby, a favorite pastime, has become an urgent need. So many have caught the fever and are in pursuit of the best of the sport, competitive and fierce. It's like everything else today— supply and the best from the everyday to the rarest.

It gets harder to find that special piece. We have discovered that there are others who feel just as we do that one of something is never enough. The necessity to corner the market is the true sign of the passionate obsessive collector . . . more is always better. A few will never do. There is always the worry that someone will get there first. It's the trophy. But it need not be only something old.

We have met people who collect trees, cars, watches, books, teddy bears, chairs, buttons, and just about anything you can think of! Sometimes the passion of collecting is a result of trying to decorate your summer house. It could begin with the color blue of the sea and sky. Then you realize blue looks even better with lots of blues and grows more exciting when layered on. You are in the country and the inspiration of rural America is strong. New fabrics feel stiff, new furniture too perfect. Authenticity and integrity become more important than the perfect size and the matched color. It's all in the mix. No one wants a cookie-cutter look—unless it's cookie cutters you are collecting! Serious money may have been spent on dressing up a Hamptons house, but it can easily look "down home" and have a feel-rich decorating scheme.

Everyone has their personalized style. It's all in the details and the ultimate detail is collecting. There is a couple we know who has many collecting interests, although they also have their own separate pursuits. He buys paintings, sprinklers from the thirties and forties, and has amassed a tree collection that is more extensive than your local nursery. She has stacks of brown-and-white transferware platters, shirting quilts, gladiola

PREVIOUS SPREAD: Yesterday's doorstops made from discarded materials: used milk bottles were filled with pebbles and covered with colorful scraps of fabric stuffed and shaped into dolls. Each doll is as different as the person who created her.

Eggcentric! A hard-to-find collection of various eggs makes for a very unusual collection.

vases, and a flotilla of pond boats. Together they built an extraordinary collection that complements one another. A friend of ours is another "serious collector"—his biggest problem is knowing when to stop and if he can't stop then it's knowing what to leave out. Running out of room is what collectors fear most. Pick through his shed and it's a treasure trove of good stuff. The more he stockpiles the better he feels. Don't ever ask to buy or trade—that's out of the question. Another obsessive collector whose home we visited has a transferware collection second to none, rivaled by the varied tramp art pieces displayed throughout her home. The endless collections of well-chosen objects are so carefully displayed that each area is an education in itself. Her obsessive collecting is so vast that even after many visits it's hard to see it all. Upon leaving you know you want to return.

The obsession of collecting is more than the sum of its parts. It surpasses accumulating. What is in evidence is the collector's eye. Each chosen piece is outstanding and each wonderful object reflects the personalized taste of its owner. More is more. More is better. Priceless clutter is the ultimate obsession.

A collection of old bottles that begs the usual question: How were they filled? All handmade and all eclectic—a wooden chair, an assortment of tools, a ladder, a piece of wood, pinwheels, even men sitting at a table playing cards and drinking beer. The maker is unknown but the bottles probably date back to the early 1900s. (Certainly before the age of television.)

The owner of this collection, whose passion is American folk art, lives in this gem of a 17th-century Bridgehampton village house, with the oldest part originally a blacksmith shop. Examples of wooden razors, most likely used in store displays, share a counter with a real birdhouse and boot spurs.

Duck decoys in a hand-carved box by a local craftsman from Sag Harbor.

RIGHT: These collectors can never stop at a few. A fabulous collection of water sprinklers from the 1930s and 40s covers the floor and several shelves. All are in working condition and used even today. The fourth shelf is a collection of ships in bottles. The top shelf holds a Victorian flower vase collection—the first purchase cost $1.50.

A collection of turn-of-the-century shaving mugs began when this owner was a child who proudly bought his first mug for 5¢.
They are displayed on glass shelves in such a way that they appear to go on forever.

One is never enough! Bootjacks were a necessity a long time ago. They were as practical as they were decorative and were designed in the shapes of bugs, animals, or women's bodies. The tabletop is covered with a collection of children's toys, platters, and a golden cow once used as a weathervane.

The owner of these cow signs loves this bovine creature. The tin sign collection is only a tease of what else exists on the subject. The painting above is her impression of the Library of Congress in Washington, D.C.

The owner of this transferware collection truly believes that more is better. Well displayed on a 19th-century English pine cupboard.

A collection of mainly American pottery is displayed on a wonderful example of painted American furniture. The orange drink dispenser shares a corner with a little girl whose hat is actually a lawn sprinkler.

LEFT: Tidiness counts: bowls, cake stands, metal colanders stacked high, copper pots, glass pitchers. Obsession is an understatement!

A cook's kitchen complete with double sinks supports a beautiful collection of transferware pitchers.

In the same kitchen an endless collection of McCoy pottery watches over dozens of flea market bowls and platters.

OPPOSITE: A welcoming sight! A painted blue wicker table found in Palm Beach sets the stage for the lamps, tramp art display cabinet, and other odd bits. One of a pair of Texas horn chairs anchors the still life.

An 1870 American folk art cabinet holds a beautiful collection of McCoy and Roseville pottery. The painting is by an artist named Braun from the Ashcan school of painting.

Hats, hats, and more hats . . . a well-used collection
owned by a well-known clothing designer.

More than just a home display, this pile of dyed vintage lace and linen shawls
makes you want to grab one as you leave for the evening.

The Adirondack smoking stand: colorful log cabin houses with detachable roofs sit atop little tables made during the 1930s and 40s. The charmingly fashioned rustic tables were intended to hold smoking paraphernalia and a drinking glass.

The great American woody wagon.

BELOW: A caravan of vintage trucks on their way to the garage.

home is where
the art is

Artists are always influenced by their surroundings, and in the Hamptons even more so. For close to two hundred years, artists have come here because of the vast sky, the beautiful beaches, the sea, the unspoiled rural landscape, and, of course, the light. This tradition began with William Merritt Chase and Childe Hassam and continued through the years with such memorable names as Fairfield Porter, Sheridan Lord, Roy Lichtenstein, Willem de Kooning, Jackson Pollock, Lee Krasner, Alphonso Ossorio, and right up to the present with such celebrated names as Chuck Close, Audrey Flack, Ross Bleckner, Jane Freilicher, Jane Wilson, Eric Fischl, April Gornick, and Robert Dash. The list is endless.

PREVIOUS SPREAD: Galatea, Islandia, and 2 overscaled Daphne sculptures in the Easthampton studio of sculptor Audrey Flack.

Creativity is a fragile art in and of itself, and out on the East End artists need their surroundings as fuel and inspiration. As the soulful background elements for making art, the Hamptons offer any artist a resource of extraordinary wonders—the morning mist, the sun rising and setting at the beach, the star-filled night sky. (Compared to the city, a Hamptons sky at night is a light-filled gallery of constellations and shooting stars.)

Although most of us think of paintings and sculpture when we hear the word *art*, it can just as easily include putting pen to paper or shovel to dirt. On their days off, artists paint their gardens with the same channeled energy that they do their work. It's the artist without a canvas. It's the artist at play. Others show off their culinary talents in the kitchen. Some play musical instruments. All of them earned our respect and admiration.

A house in the Hamptons is the perfect setting for creativity. The medium that artists use to express themselves may differ, but the influence of the Hamptons is the common denominator they all find so appealing. Artists have a tendency to work at odd hours. So it is a luxury to have your studio in your home and a bigger luxury to have your home in the Hamptons. Here, at home, is where the art is.

An eclectic collection of pictures, props, and human figures in Audrey Flack's studio.

Long-time Sagaponack resident Susan Meisel paints with a whimsical design and a happy palette.

LEFT: Steve Miller's studio in Sagaponack.

Artists' tools.

RIGHT: The studio of landscape painter Susan Nash in Bridgehampton.

A masterpiece in progress in the studio of Chuck Close.

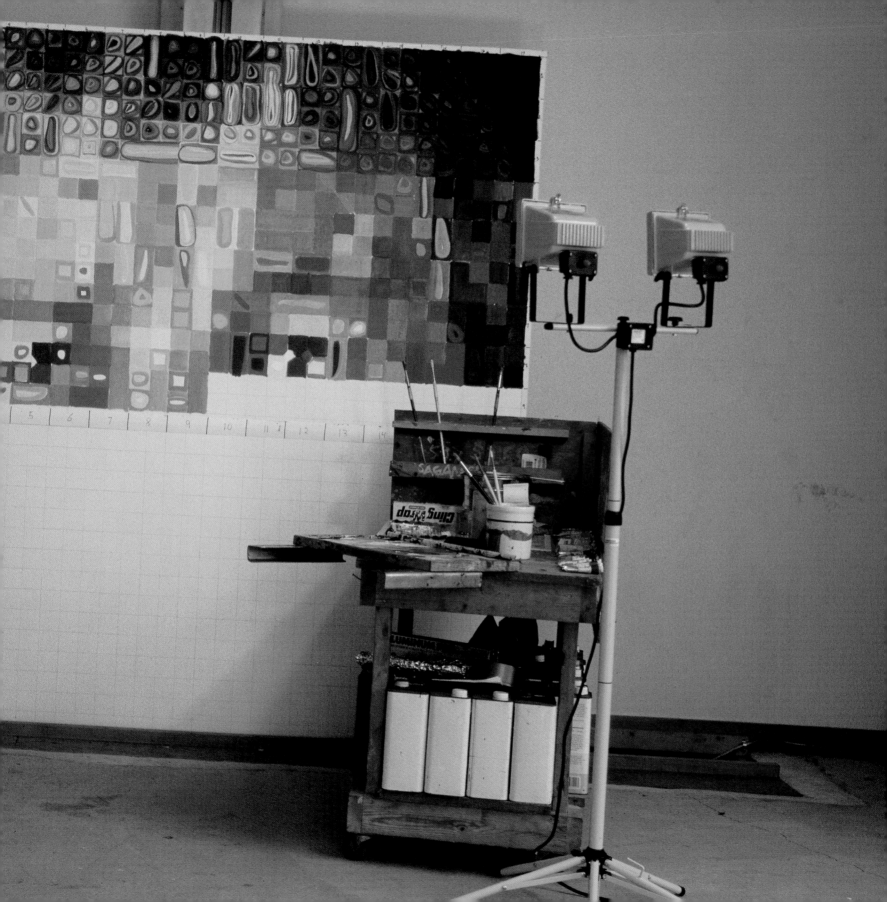

Ross Bleckner's studio in Sagaponack was a later addition to this home once owned by Truman Capote.

The grande dame of the Hamptons landscape, Jane Freilicher, has lived and worked in Watermill for over 20 years.

LEFT: *Blue Rings* by California sculptor Jerome Kirk is a 9-foot-high painted aluminum mobile in Sagaponack Field.

ABOVE: *Home Land,* a patinated bronze sculpture by New York artist Oded Halahmy, in Sagaponack Sculpture Field.

RIGHT: *Civitas* by Audrey Flack is a 16-foot-high bronze sculpture.

as good
as it gets

This picture-perfect place known as the Hamptons validates the all-American style. We are continually moved by the turn-of-the-century shingled cottages, the few remaining elm-lined village roads, and the tranquility that prevails. It's the simple order of things. The big sky and the flat land create a portrait clearer than a landscape painter's brush. The blue sea and panoramic views calm us as we rest on bleached white sand beaches or set sail on the open sea. All of these qualities "say" that luxury is a state of mind. No matter if it is a little shack or a compound that you are staying in, or even if you are just visiting friends for the weekend, you can still be seduced into enjoying all the Hamptons have to offer. Whether biking, walking, or driving, the fields of sunflowers, the straight rows of corn, and tall hedges never fail to please the eye. The nighttime big sky with millions of stars, the sound of the ocean, and the fresh smell in the air never stop making you feel that this is all possibly as good as it gets. Yes, it's a postcard view, it's a bucolic dream that's even better because it is real. It is the end of a perfect day. It's as good as it gets. Who could ask for more?

Manicured boxwood balls frame the way to this perfectly tended garden path.

PREVIOUS SPREAD: From this front porch generations have been blessed with one of the best settings for a great view and summer breezes.

The All-American early 1900s cottage.

Shingled and graceful is this doyenne of good taste on the simply named but famous Lily Pond Lane.

Memories of childhood.

This charming Easthampton cottage looks like it could be in the countryside in England.

A vintage wooden Chris Craft.

OPPOSITE: Perfect in design—a great Shelter Island boat house.

BELOW: . . . And suddenly it's summer.

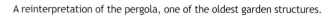

A reinterpretation of the pergola, one of the oldest garden structures.

RIGHT: This weekend family home in Watermill has a unique way of creating a tentlike effect for dinner parties. On a breezy evening the curtains are let loose and provide an exotic atmosphere.

The calming effect of a reflecting pool makes one linger at this formal Southampton garden.

A secret garden in a Watermill garden.

RIGHT: An allee of old Easthampton Elms.

An Easthampton summerhouse complete with its own outdoor meditation room.

This setting speaks for itself . . . Breathtaking comes to mind.

OVERLEAF: As good as it gets.